A Prologue To Her Silence

One Girl. One Pen. Twenty-One Steps to Becoming.

Karthika S Babu

Made with ❤ on the BookLeaf Publishing Platform
www.bookleafpub.in
www.bookleafpub.com

Dedication

To the girl I was, quiet, hurting, and lost in her own silence. This is your voice, finally heard.

And to every soul who ever felt like the darkness would win, may these pages remind you: you are not alone, and you are not finished.

Preface

This is the story of a girl who learned to write her pain and, in doing so, discovered the power of survival. Through twenty-one poems, you will walk with her through darkness, desperation, and despair. You will feel her silence, her fear, and her loneliness—as she does, trapped within her own thoughts, searching for a way out.

But this is also the story of hope. Each poem is a step toward healing, a reflection of the strength it takes to rise again after everything has fallen apart. You will witness her transformation, not just from grief to joy, but from void of self doubt to the fullness of self love. In every verse, there's a reminder that even in the quietest of moments, the loudest strength can be found.

It is the story of reclaiming a life, piece by fragile piece—one word at a time. For anyone who has ever felt lost, for anyone who has ever wondered if they could go on, this collection is for you. There is no ending here. Only a beginning. And in the pages of this book, you will see that nothing is beyond repair, and nothing is too broken to be made whole.

Acknowledgements

This collection was born from a place I once feared I would never return from—a space of silence, of struggle, of nearly giving up. But poetry gave me a lifeline. Words became a way out, and eventually, a way forward.

To my family, friends and loved ones, thank you for holding space for me—even when I didn't know how to ask. Your quiet presence was louder than anything I could say.

To every reader who picks up this book, I see you. I wrote this for you, for all the things you've felt and could not explain. May these poems feel like a mirror, a friend, or a whisper in the dark reminding you to keep going.

And lastly, to healing—thank you for being patient with me.

1. The Weight of Silence

I wake, but don't rise—
just sink deeper into the mattress,
into the hush that clings
to my bones like wet clothes.

The walls have forgotten my voice,
and maybe I have too.
There's a scream curled in my throat
that never learned to leave.

My thoughts come in whispers,
scared of their own shadow.
Even they tiptoe around me,
afraid to speak too loud.

I eat in silence.
I sit in silence.
I cry so softly
even the night doesn't hear me.

They say it's sadness—
but it feels more like absence.
Not pain, exactly.
More like... being erased.

The mirror avoids my eyes.
Even the glass can't bear to reflect
someone who's fading
from the inside out.

I scroll through days like pages
in a book I didn't choose,
each one blank,
each one heavy with meaninglessness.

I write nothing. I speak less.
But the silence is loud—
a constant hum,
a hymn of things I can't say.

They say time heals.
I think time just learns to look away.
And I've learned, too—
how to vanish without leaving the room.

2. Drowning in the Daylight

There's a throb beneath the silence,
not loud, not sharp — just there.
Like a breath held too long
or a question left unanswered.

Everyone else seems to bloom
when the morning breaks.
The world glows gold.
But I... I wilt.

The sun touches my skin,
but it never reaches inside.
It only lights up
the hollow I try to hide.

Laughter spills down the street
like music I forgot how to dance to.
I watch from a window
with curtains half-drawn —
not open enough to live,

not closed enough to escape.

They say "You look fine,"
but they don't see how
my smile is stitched
with invisible thread
and barely holds.

I don't remember
what it feels like to belong
in a world that moves so fast
when I can barely stand still.

I breathe, but it burns.
I wake, but I ache.
And the cruelest thing is—
no one sees a girl drowning
when it's daylight.

3. When the Mirror Turned Away

The mirror has grown indifferent—
it no longer flinches at my gaze.
It reflects a silhouette draped in skin,
but none of her edges feel like mine.

Her eyes are fogbound windows,
haunted by a thousand silent sonnets,
where once a spark resided—
now, only embers bruised with dusk.

I mouth old names to summon her,
but they collapse, weightless,
against the glass.
Even my voice sounds foreign now—
a ghost rehearsing lines
from a life I no longer inhabit.

She moves as I move,
yet I sense the distance.

An actress in borrowed light,
trapped in the theater of reflection,
reciting grief without applause.

Who is she—this paper soul
unfolding quietly into the quiet?

Perhaps I left myself
in the margin of a forgotten morning,
and the mirror, weary of lies,
has turned away
to mourn me in its silence.

4. The Night She Let Go

It was not darkness that frightened her—
but the stillness.
A stillness so profound
it pressed against her lungs
like a final breath waiting to be released.

The moon hung like a witness
outside the window,
silent, silver,
watching her unmake herself
in trembling increments.

She sat with her knees drawn to her chest,
folded like a letter never sent,
a confession inked in invisible grief.

The walls knew.
The silence knew.
And somewhere beneath her ribs,
her soul curled inward,

craving an ending
that didn't ache so loudly.

She thought of peace—
not the kind sung about in lullabies,
but the kind that sleeps beneath soil,
untouched,
unbothered by mornings
that demand too much.

She imagined absence
like a soft exhale—
a slipping out of self
as seamless as shadow departing light.

Her fingertips hovered over the edge
of a decision too sharp to name,
and time held its breath,
unsure if it would still exist
on the other side of her silence.

But just as she leaned into the ache,
something stopped her—
not a thunderclap of hope,
but a thread.
Delicate. Trembling.
Still tethered to the world

by the thinnest string of maybe.

Maybe someone would miss her.
Maybe this wasn't the end.
Maybe—
and in that maybe,
a flicker of her breath remembered
how to return.

5. Almost Gone

She stood on the edge of everything
and listened to the wind—
it spoke in voices
she had long forgotten.

She wasn't crying,
though the tears were close.
She wasn't screaming,
but her heart had forgotten
how to stay inside her chest.

She was hollow,
empty like a house
waiting for the rain to fill it,
waiting for the silence to break.

It felt like dying,
but it also felt like peace—
a quiet kind of surrender
where nothing mattered anymore.

Not the morning,
not the sky,
not the people who loved her
from a distance
she couldn't cross.

She thought maybe it would be easier
to just let go—
let herself fall into the nothingness
and be free from this ache.

But then, a breath.
A tremor.
A single thought that whispered,
Not yet.
And for just a moment,
she stayed.
Not with strength,
not with hope—
but with the faintest echo of something
that refused to die.

6. Breathing, Barely

She did not rise like the heroines do—
not with fire,
not with fury.
She simply woke.
And that was enough to call it survival.

Her breath came in fragments,
like pages torn from an old book—
some with ink,
some with only silence.

She wasn't sure if she wanted to keep breathing,
but her body did,
out of muscle memory,
or maybe rebellion.

Each inhale was a negotiation:
a pact with pain
she hadn't agreed to sign.
But still—

her chest lifted,
her lungs obeyed.

She walked through the world
like a ghost in her own story,
touching nothing,
feeling less.
But even ghosts have shadows,
and hers still clung to her heels.

There was no poetry in her steps,
no light in her eyes.
Only the quiet proof
that she was still here—
that grief hadn't claimed her completely.

Some days, that was enough.
Some days, that was everything.

She did not speak of hope.
But breath after breath,
she carried its weight,
barely.

7. The Flicker Within

Somewhere inside the hollow of her,
where silence had built its kingdom,
a flicker stirred.
A breath not hers,
a warmth not summoned.

It didn't roar,
didn't blaze—
it whispered.

A stubborn ember,
nestled beneath the ruins,
where even despair had forgotten to look.

She touched it, timidly,
as if it might vanish at her nearness.
But it stayed.
Quivering. Trembling.
Alive.

She had been nothing for so long—
nothing but broken echoes and borrowed days.
Yet here it was,
a small defiance,
a secret vow stitched into her chest:
You are not finished yet.

She did not know how to feed it.
She only knew she could not bear to lose it.
So she cupped her broken hands around it,
and breathed.
And the flame, oh —
it breathed back.

8. Unfinished Goodbye

I tried to leave once—
tried to fold myself
into the soft forgetting of night.
I even rehearsed the goodbye,
scribbled in invisible ink
across the walls of my ribcage.

But when the hour came,
my voice fractured into silence.
And the words—
the solemn farewell I thought I could offer—
hung heavy in my mouth,
unspoken,
unfinished.

There were names I could not release,
faces stitched into my memory
with threads too stubborn to tear.

There were dreams,

half-buried under sorrow,
that reached up with trembling hands
when I tried to bury them.

And somewhere deep in the marrow of me,
something begged—
not for death,
but for a different kind of ending.

I thought surrender would be easy.
I thought vanishing would be simple.
But life clung to me
in ways I didn't understand.

Not in grand, sweeping moments—
but in the ordinary:
the way the rain touched my window,
the way the stars still blinked at me,
the way my heart, traitor that it was,
kept beating.

I never said goodbye.
Not really.
I just wept the words into my pillow
and breathed them back in before dawn.

And somehow,
the world held me anyway.

9. A Letter to the Void

Dear Nothingness,
dear hollow cathedral of my chest,
dear endless echo I mistook for silence—

I have worn your name like a second skin,
have prayed to your absence more times
than I can remember how to pray for anything else.

I am tired,
tired in ways that sleep cannot touch,
tired in places too deep for hands to reach.
I have bled invisible rivers beneath smiles,
have drowned quietly
while the world praised me for breathing.

I have given you everything—
my laughter, once wild and careless,
my dreams, once stitched in gold and wonder,
my voice, once certain it had something to say.

You swallowed them whole,
and still, you hungered for more.

You taught me how to vanish in plain sight,
how to sit in crowded rooms
and feel like a rumor.

You taught me to mistrust my own reflection,
to unmake myself each morning,
to apologize for the very air I borrowed.

And yet, despite it all—
despite the aching quiet you draped around my
shoulders—
I find myself here, still scribbling toward a dawn
I do not yet believe in.

Is that rebellion?
Is that foolishness?
Or is it the stubborn, aching ghost of hope
that refuses to yield?

I do not know.
But tonight,
as my hands tremble against the page,
I want you to know:

You almost won.
Almost.

But there are pieces of me,
fragments too small for your hunger to devour,
still clinging,
still aching,
still alive.

And they are learning, slowly,
how to love the ruins.

Sincerely,
The girl you could not keep.

10. The Sun Saw Me

I was not seeking it,
not begging the heavens for mercy.
I was simply standing there—
tired, trembling, small—
when the sun,
soft and certain,
laid its hand upon my shoulder.

It did not ask if I was worthy.
It did not flinch at the scars.
It only said,
You are still here,
and poured its golden forgiveness
into every hollow place I carried.

For a breath,
for a heartbeat,
I was not forgotten.

The world saw me—
and for once,
I let it look.
And i did not run.

11. Steps Woven from Ashes

I did not rise in triumph;
I stumbled,
barefoot across the ruins of my own undoing.

Each step was a prayer,
half-forgotten, half-born,
stitched together with trembling hands
and a heart that barely believed in mornings anymore.

The ground beneath me was still warm with sorrow,
scattered with the brittle remains of old dreams,
but I walked—
not because I was certain,
but because standing still had become another kind of
death.

My legs remembered before my mind did,
how to bend,
how to sway,
how to carry the weight of almost-letting-go

and still move forward.

I wore my fear like a second skin,
but even fear grew weary
of trying to hold me still.

The winds that once tore at me in rage
now only whispered through my hair,
brushing against my ribs
like a mother checking for breath.

I walked—
one step, then another—
across the ashes of who I had been,
threading sorrow and survival together,
weaving a life
not perfect,
not unbroken,
but mine.

And with every uncertain step,
the earth sang a little louder,
as if it, too,
had been waiting for my return.

12. Scars in Bloom

My skin is a tapestry of sorrows,
stitched with trembling hands
and nights too heavy to carry alone.

Each scar — a whispered elegy,
a testimony that the blade,
whether of grief or time,
could not wholly undo me.

For years I wore them like shame,
hiding the constellations etched across my bones,
believing that beauty belonged only
to the unbroken.

But healing is not a quiet thing,
nor is it clean.
It is riotous,
wild as vines through the ruins
of a once-sacred city,
claiming space where despair tried to reign.

And here—
here in the garden of what remains—
the scars have blossomed.

Wounds that once wept in silence
now cradle flowers in their hollowed cradles;
petals soft as forgiveness,
roots deep as memory.

I do not need to be unmarked to be holy.
I do not need to be untouched to be worthy.

The earth remembers every footprint,
even the ones that faltered.
The heart remembers every fracture,
even the ones that tried to erase it.

And I—
I remember now:
I was not broken.
I was being planted.

And today,
I bloom.

13. The Choice to Stay

It was not a thunderous decision,
not a heroic cry carved into the bones of mountains.
It was quiet.
A trembling breath taken against the weight of every
ghost
that told me to surrender.

I sat there, on the crumbling ledge of myself,
the abyss humming its ancient lullaby beneath my feet,
and I listened—
to the ache,
to the longing,
to the tired hope that refused to die.

Stay,
the world whispered,
through the cracks in the window,
through the weary hum of my own heart.
Stay—
not because it will be easy,

but because somewhere, within the wreckage,
there are gardens yet to be found.

I chose not certainty,
nor even happiness—
but the sacred, defiant act
of wanting to see what happens next.

I chose the slow, stubborn architecture of healing.
I chose the tiny rebellions:
another breath,
another step,
another dream rebuilt from splinters.

I chose to stay—
to stay with my brokenness,
to stay with my unfinished songs,
to stay with the unbearable beauty of beginnings.

And though the darkness pressed its palms against my
back,
though the past howled for my return,
I turned my face toward the wind,
and stayed.

Not because I was fearless.
Not because I was unscarred.

But because even the wounded
can love the sky.

14. Hope in Strange Places

I thought hope would come dressed in gold,
in grand symphonies and sun-drenched promises.
I thought it would be loud, undeniable,
a banner unfurling across my broken sky.

But it came quieter than that—
a single blade of green
curling through the fractures of a place I had long
abandoned.

Hope came not to the polished rooms of my heart,
but to the forgotten corridors,
to the dust-choked corners where sorrow had built its
altars.

It found me in the smallest mercies—
the warmth of a stranger's fleeting smile,
the stubborn bloom of a flower clawing through
concrete,
the sacred way morning insisted on returning,

even when I had not asked it to.

Hope came as a rebellion,
soft but unyielding,
a hand slipping into mine when I believed I was
unholdable.

It taught me that survival is stitched together
from unnoticed graces—
a breath you almost didn't take,
a tear you finally let fall,
a laugh that escapes you when you thought you had
forgotten how.

It taught me that you do not have to be ready for hope to
find you.
You only have to be alive.
And sometimes, that is enough.

15. Love Found me Anyway

I did not call for it.
I was too busy burying parts of myself
beneath silence and apology.

Love arrived not as fire,
nor storm,
but as the quiet hum beneath my grief—
soft as dusk,
brave as breath.

It stepped gently over broken things,
ran its fingers along the dust of who I'd been,
and whispered,
Even now, you are worthy.

I warned it:
I am rusted through with sorrow,
I am stitched from old fears
and half-spoken goodbyes.

But it didn't flinch.
Didn't try to fix or soften me.
It simply stayed—
a presence,
a pause,
a steady warmth against my trembling.

Love came not to save me,
but to see me—
in the raw,
in the ruin,
in the sacred wreckage of who I was becoming.

And in that gaze,
I began to see myself again.
Not polished,
not perfect—
but profoundly held.

16. The Arms That Held Me

There are arms,
somewhere beyond the ache,
that do not tremble at the weight of your sorrow.

There are hands,
not here to fix,
not here to erase,
but simply to gather the pieces you thought were too
broken to touch.

I fell—
not gracefully,
not with the poise of survival songs,
but like autumn crumbles into winter,
with the exhausted sigh of something that has held on
too long.

And there—
in the brittle hush of almost-letting-go—
arms found me.

They did not demand an explanation.
They did not ask me to be anything other than a
breathing, breaking thing.

They became a sanctuary made of skin and forgiveness,
a shelter where the storms inside me could beat against
ribs
without being turned away.

In those arms,
I learned that collapse was not failure—
it was a language too.

It said:
Stay.
Come undone if you must.
You are still loved.

And somewhere, pressed against that wordless mercy,
I wept.
I surrendered.
I remembered how it felt
to be human
and held
at the same time.

17. Learning to Rise Again

I did not rise like the phoenix —
there was no fire,
no spectacle of ash turned to glory.
I rose like a wilted flower
learning again how to stretch toward light.

With limbs stiff from forgetting,
with lungs hesitant to trust the air,
I performed the oldest ritual known to the wounded:
I stood.

The earth beneath me did not cheer.
The sky did not open its arms.
But my shadow shifted —
and that was enough.

This was not triumph.
This was not beauty in the way poets often promise.
This was survival wrapped in the quiet silk of trying,
a resurrection that whispered, not roared.

My spine, once curled in grief,
remembered the language of upright.
My hands, once made of tremble,
reached for their own weight
and carried it.

There is an art
to rising while still broken—
to standing with your splinters
and saying, this, too, is me.

So I crowned myself
with dust and defiance,
and walked barefoot across the threshold
of another fragile morning.

And though my scars chimed like windchimes in the
hush,
I did not silence them.
They were my bells—
my proof that I had been to the edge
and brought my name back with me.

18. Giving What I Needed

Once, I was a house
with no open windows,
no hands knocking gently on the door.
Only echoes,
and the wish
that someone might notice the quiet collapse
behind my smile.

I starved for softness—
not the kind wrapped in noise,
but the kind that whispers,
You don't have to explain your ache to be held.

No one came quite like that.
But now—
I do.

I arrive where the silence is thick,
where eyes look away too quickly,
and I stay.

I do not rush the sorrow.
I do not name the pain.
I simply offer my presence
like a warm shawl
for someone else's storm.

I have learned to become
what I once begged the universe to send me.

To the shaking hands,
I offer stillness.
To the lost,
I offer light without direction—
just enough glow to remind them
they're not walking alone.

This is how grace moves:
not in thunder,
but in the mercy we make
from our own shattered altars.

And as I give,
a soft, sacred thing unfurls in me—
the quiet knowledge
that healing is not always found
in being saved,

but in becoming the sanctuary
you once prayed for.

19. Lit from the Ruins

Once, she knelt beneath storms
with palms turned upward,
pleading skyward
for any god
to hold her.

Now—
she is the quiet chapel
built from the rubble
of unanswered prayers.

She does not speak in thunder anymore,
but in hush—
in the language of lamplight,
of kettle-steam and open doors.

She learned to steep warmth
from sorrow,
to braid the ache
into blankets for others.

Where she once wept into the wind,
she now listens
like an old tree listens—
still,
but holding
a thousand storms in her bark.

She does not rescue.
She does not preach.
She simply stays.

She offers her presence
like wild honey—
slow, golden,
and without demand.

This is not the love she was given—
but the love she became
when the world
grew too loud
and no one stayed.

Now,
when she sees another
crack beneath the weight of breath,
she does not turn away.

She becomes the soft place
where sorrow may sleep,
where grief is named
and not shamed.

She is the hearth.
The hush.
The hand that reaches back.

She is the shelter
she once begged for.

And she is not waiting
to be thanked.

20. Nothing Ends Here

They said the world ends
in a silence too wide for words,
in the weight of doors closing,
in the ache of hands letting go.

But they were wrong.

The world ends,
and then it sighs into beginning again.

I was a girl who mistook falling
for finality—
who stitched farewell
into the hem of every sorrow.

But sorrow, too, is a seam
that can be unstitched.
Even graves grow gardens
if left long enough to the rain.

Nothing ends here.
Not the soft pulse beneath broken ribs,
not the faint hymn of breath
threading itself into morning.

I am the aftermath that bloomed.
I am the ruin that chose to rise.
I am the question
still daring to be asked.

I have buried countless yesterdays
with trembling hands,
yet here I stand—
not unbroken,
but unbowed.

Nothing ends here.
Only beginnings wear the mask of endings
until we are brave enough
to call them otherwise.

21. A Prologue to Her Silence

She no longer writes in thunder.
She writes in stillness now—
in breath,
in glances,
in the way she chooses to stay.

Once, her silence was absence.
Now, it is memory—
a garden grown from grief,
each stem a word
she no longer needs to speak aloud.

She has wept in the language of rain,
bled in the ink of longing,
and risen—
not to be loud,
but to be whole.

The world did not end.

It bent,
it broke,
and still,
she stood.

So let her silence not be mistaken
for emptiness—
it is a language beyond grief,
a hymn without sound,
a quiet that remembers
everything.

And if you meet her in passing,
do not ask for her story.
Just notice
how even the wind
bows gently
when she walks by.

The quiet you bear
is not void,
but vessel.
It is the sacred hush
where becoming begins.

You are not the silence.
You are the voice

that returned from it
wreathed in light.